unbiased advice from the animal kingdom

critter wisdom for humans

susan rutledge

WILLOW
BEND
PRESS

Published by Willow Bend Press, Prosper, TX
willowbendpress.com
Hardcover ISBN-13: 978-1-950019-14-4
Paperback ISBN-13: 978-1-950019-15-1
First Printing April 2020
Author: Susan Rutledge
www.susanrutledge.com
Front Cover photograph by David Clode
Back Cover photograph by Andre Mouton

Publisher's Cataloging-in-Publication Data

Name: Rutledge, Susan, author.
Title: Critter wisdom for humans : unbiased advice from the animal kingdom / Susan Rutledge.
Description: Prosper, TX: Willow Bend Press, 2020.
Identifiers: ISBN: 978-1-950019-14-4 (Hardcover) | 978-1-950019-15-1 (pbk.)
Subjects: LCSH Conduct of life--Quotations, maxims, etc. | Animals--Pictorial works. | Pets--Pictorial works. | BISAC SELF-HELP / Personal Growth / General
Classification: LCC PN6084.C556 R88 2020 | DDC 082--dc23

for more books by Susan Rutledge
go to
susanrutledge.com

mind
your own
monkey
business

make sure you
can swim
before you're
in over
your head

play nice
so no one
gets hurt

get out
of the nest
and spread
your wings

pouting never
gets you
anywhere

look at circumstances from other points of view

if you don't have
a thing to wear...
do your
laundry

be kind to
everyone...
even if
they don't look
like you

don't hide
from
your mistakes

do life
with a friend

grab a
parachute
before
you jump

learn to
be quiet
and listen

take off
the mask...
you be you

stick your
neck out
and
go for it

just because
it's in style
doesn't mean
it's right for you

feed your brain...
read a book

look for
happiness
on your side
of the fence

don't waste
life
staring at a
screen

wrinkles
eventually
happen

find
someone
to love

don't look
back
with regret...
live with
purpose

hold on
to the ones
you love

there will be
bad hair days...
invest in a
ball cap

carrying
life's baggage
slows
you down

appreciate
the world
around you

go big
or
go home

getting
all puffed up
is never pretty

accessories
make the
difference

stick
together...
family is
important

smile big
and remember
to brush
your teeth

give
comfort
and
show
affection

control
your
tongue

staring
is just
plain rude

pretending
to be
invisible
never works

keep
climbing
and don't
look down

look for
the prince
in every
frog

face your fears

honesty
is as simple
as black
and white

look
people
in the eye

be content
with who
you see
in the mirror

seriously...
laugh
often

make
good choices
so you can
hold your
head high

saying "I'm sorry"
is not a sign
of weakness

break through
barriers
and follow
your dreams

be patient,
your time
is
coming

hugs are
good
for the heart

make
the most
of each
day

www.ingramcontent.com/pod-product-compliance
Lightning Source LLC
Chambersburg PA
CBHW041540260326
41914CB00015B/1512